A Journal for the Generations:

Equipping Your Future With Wisdom from the Past

References for Scripture Quotations

ISBN –978-1-953788-39-9 (Printed)

Amber C. Blakes, M.Ed.

A Journal for the Generations:

Equipping Your Future With Wisdom from the Past

I dedicate this book to my Grandma Arrabelle (Arra) Lane, who sat me down as a teenager and talked to me about being respectful to my parents. She has continued to share so much more wisdom with me throughout the rest of my life. I regret not writing it all down to pass her wisdom down to my children. For this reason, I've penned this journal to record some of my journey for my children, grandchildren, and great-grandchildren to enjoy and benefit from.

Acknowledgments

I'm grateful to God for being patient with me and giving me a tremendous amount of grace. I'll forever be thankful to my mom, Marn, who instilled a love of reading and books in me at a very young age and has encouraged me every step of the way. Thank you to my sister, Shavonne, and my many sisters in Christ who have prayed for or pushed me into purpose. Many thanks to the writing coaches with Beyond the Book Media for guiding me through the process of completing my first manuscript. I'm so thankful to my children, Ayana, Isaiah, and Amina, for providing the motivation I needed to persevere through conquering the new territory of becoming an author. Finally, I couldn't have done this without my amazing husband Irving's sacrifices and unconditional love, understanding, and support. I'm beyond grateful for the system support that God has chosen to love me through. I pray that each person who touches this book is blessed with a circle of people who enthusiastically believe in and support them.

TABLE OF CONTENTS

Introduction:
Fighting for Your Posterity and The Forward Progress of Future Generations

"My people are ruined because they don't know what's right or true." Hosea 4:6 MSG

For as long as I can remember, I wanted to be a wife and a mother. I don't remember having any other dreams for my life that were so sure and God-ordained. I've earned two degrees and a variety of certifications in my career. I've traveled and have had great friendships. I've written a variety of pieces and sang in choirs. I've presented professionally to my colleagues time and time again. But when asked what I dream of being or doing, I could only definitively say I wanted to be a wife and a mother. Admittedly, that answer seemed to be noble but common and not great. I no longer question the significance of my calling and now know that these are the only two roles God needed me to fulfill to focus on in this life because from these positions, I would become a generation blesser and curse breaker for my family's bloodline.

Early in life, I realized that God had blessed me with cognitive and emotional intelligence, an insatiable desire to learn, and a conviction to share what I knew with the masses. I believed that documenting what I'd learned throughout life would help my family and others break free from years of bondage and walk into blessings that can help them experience financial freedom and total wholeness. Take heed to this admonishment: what God shows you isn't just for you. It is for you to set others free, bring revenue back into your house, and leave a legacy for future generations.

I've also written this journal to be used as a tool by you and countless others who want to leave behind a record of their words and the heart behind them for future generations to benefit from beyond the days we live on the Earth. It is also a tool to equip your children, their children, and other family members to live victoriously over the struggles and cyclical patterns you and your ancestors have struggled with. This journal will also allow you to share what you've learned about the most important topics in life. You can also pass on the gifts, talents, and strengths that run in your family so your future generations will know and can believe in the possibility of carrying on those successes in their own lives. With this journal in hand, your posterity won't have to wonder why they think the way they think, struggle with certain challenges and excel at certain talents. Because of what you share in this journal, they can approach a life full of unknowns knowing what the shoulders they stand on dealt with, struggled with, or overcame.

More importantly, continuing this tradition of passing down documented personal struggles, lessons, successes, and resources has the potential to break the vicious cyclical patterns of struggle for your family. You want to see your family go from success to more success and believe and hope each generation can be and do better than the generation before them, and now you possess a tool to help you do just that.

Ultimately, what you are reading is a guide to facilitate the eradication of the Success-Struggle-Success Pattern for your family. None of us want to see our children do worse than us or wonder if our grandchildren will be successful. If what you include within is honestly communicated and passed on at the right time, it can result in your family building upon each other's successes for generations to come.

How to Use This Journal

A Journal for the Generations is intended to be a keepsake to be passed down and written in through three generations and read by the fourth generation and beyond.

"So, go now and write all this down. Put it in a book So that the record will be there to instruct the coming generations," Isaiah 30:8 MSG

Write your entries as the first generation to document what you want to pass on with the person from the second generation in mind that you will pass this journal on to. They will read what you've written from the first generation and add to it from the second generation. Then they will pass this journal on to their chosen recipient from the third generation, who will also add their wisdom and pass it on to a family member in the fourth generation to read and learn from. This fulfills the mandate given in Deuteronomy 5:9:

"You must not bow down to them or worship them, for I, the LORD your God, am a jealous God who will not tolerate your affection for any other gods. I lay the sins of the parents upon their children; the entire family is affected—even children in the third and fourth generations of those who reject me." Deuteronomy 5:9 NLT

As the saying goes, knowledge is power. There is a comfort and sense of belonging that comes with knowing about your family's experiences when you are processing the hand life has dealt you. Imagine having words of wisdom from your parents, grandparents, and/or great grandparents to guide you when you are searching for your purpose in life, choosing someone to marry, or becoming a parent for the first time. This is the gift that this journal will allow you to pass along.

For those that will have this journal passed on to them, it's my sincere prayer that you return here often, read the words within this book, and record your own journey. The entries will have different meanings to you at different seasons in life. You will have more to add with each new life experience.

How wonderful if you can benefit by knowing what your family has overcome, but it's even better if you add your experiences and pass that on to the younger members of your family. This pathway of communication is how to break cycles of regression and ensure that your family makes progress with each generation.

Section 1: Being God's Child

What about God? How do I navigate life with Him? When do I spend time with Him? Why do I need God? Who is He to me? Where do I find Him?

Jesus.

Everything begins here and with Him. Ultimately, God the Father will want to know what you did with the opportunity to know His Son and introduce Him to others. This is the one and only thing you cannot do life without. Jesus, and all that He has accomplished, must be the cornerstone of your life. You build your life upon Him and all that He has done. Believe in Him, read about Him in the Bible, pray in His name, listen to what He speaks to your heart, write what He says down, tell others about Him, and follow His example. He is your everything, and if you have a willing heart to find Him, He will meet you where you are and change you for the better.

Relationship.

Imagine meeting someone, getting to know them, and deciding this person would be worth having in your life as a friend. You spend more time and develop your relationship with them. One day they save your life from a tragic accident. Maybe they save you from drowning or pull you from burning wreckage. After that, you know that this person is a true friend for life. You go through life telling everyone that they are your friend, how great they are, and what they did for you, but you never spend time with them or get to know what is going on with them. Would you stay friends? Or would you just have a story to tell about what they once did for you?

Time.

You must spend time with God as often as you can, or else He will begin to feel like that friend you can talk about but are not really in a relationship with. You need Him because He created you and knows you better than anyone, including you. Go to a place where you can close the door and be alone with Him. Get to know every facet of Him. Talk freely to Him and listen to Him carefully. Read His word and pray it back to Him. Take note of everything He tells you, and do what He says. Find a church community that teaches the truth about God and His word and be active there. When you act on the instructions He gives, you will become a powerful force on the Earth. Do what He says, and believe what He says will happen for you.

What do you want to share with the next generation about how to navigate life with God?

To the one whom this is passed on to, what do you want to share with the next generation about how to navigate life with God?

To the next one whom this is passed on to, what do you want to share with the next generation about how to navigate life with God?

Section 2:
Being a Friend

How important are friendships? How do I create and maintain friendships? Why do I need friendships? What type of friend should I look for and be? When do I end a friendship?

Others.

Family is important, but you need friends. Friendships can be complicated, but they are necessary. Let God lead you to the right friends and steer you away from the wrong ones. Strive to be friendly and pay attention to the people who are important to you. Communicate with others often, honestly, and lovingly. Make an effort to reach out to friends even if they don't reach out to you. Respond to those who make an effort to reach out to you. When you realize you were wrong, apologize.

When you find people worth spending time with apart from your time with God and family, be good to and easy on them. Always search for the why behind what people do and say. Don't be easily offended. When you feel offended, give it to God and forgive quickly. Offense and unforgiveness are destiny killers, so do not let them into your life through your friendships. Be kind with your words. Be wise about setting boundaries that protect your energy and peace when people prove that they are not good friends. Ask God to keep you healed and whole in your heart and mind so that you're a friend from a healthy place.

Seasons.

Some friendships will not last forever. It's ok to keep in touch, but not be close friends anymore. It's ok to love others from a distance. It may feel sad when a friendship changes or when a friend becomes friends with someone else. It's natural to feel this way, but don't allow that to wound your soul. Wish them well and focus on God, yourself, and family relationships while believing that God will bring new friends into your life.

Self.

To be a good friend, you must learn to be your own friend. Learn your preferences, what you like and don't like, and enjoy what makes you happy. Spend some time alone doing what brings your soul joy. Enjoy outdoor beauty, read great literature, listen to music, sing & dance, exercise, travel, watch a good movie or show, shop, or explore your surroundings. Do these things solo! Remember, being alone doesn't mean you are lonely. Get to know and like yourself, which will put you in a great position to be a wonderful friend.

What do you want to share with the next generation about how to navigate friendships throughout life?

To the one whom this is passed on to, what do you want to share with the next generation about how to navigate friendships throughout life?

To the next one whom this is passed on to, what do you want to share with the next generation about how to navigate friendships through life?

Section 3:
Being a Student

Why is getting an education so important?
How do I make learning work for me?
How do I overcome when school seems too hard, or I fail?

Learn.

Being taught is a privilege, and this blessing deserves your effort in return. Look at and listen to your teachers, leaders, pastors, and mentors when they are speaking. Ask them questions when you don't understand or want to know more. Converse with them about your thoughts and connections to what they are teaching. Write down what they say and study it. Read everything that you can. Never stop learning. Sharing your learning so others may benefit is why getting an education is so important. Show evidence of your learning by writing or speaking beautifully and concisely about what you've learned. Create something from your new learning and make your learning visible by creating content. This will give you an edge over others and allow you to offer what you know to those who need it.

Grow.

Personal growth is essential. When measuring how much you've grown over time, only compare yourself to yourself. Each day, do something to work towards getting better than you were yesterday. Make goals based on where you are and build from there. Measure your current progress against your former progress. Comparing yourself to others is dangerous, so don't do it. Never stop growing.

Passion & Calling.

Ask God often and early on in life what He placed you on Earth to accomplish. Take risks and try new things. Notice what motivates you and speaks to the passion in you. Work towards learning and improving at your calling while you're still in school rather than waiting until you've graduated. Make gathering new skills a lifelong journey so that you become and stay excellent at what you're passionate about and called to do. It's been said that your passion is what you would do for free, but doing it for income hardly feels like work.

What do you want the next generation to know about school, being a student, and learning?

To the one whom this is passed on to, what do you want the next generation to know about school, being a student, and learning?

To the next one whom this is passed on to, what do you want the next generation to know about school, being a student, and learning?

Section 4:
Being in Business of Work & Life

How do I make money? Where am I meant to work? What do I do with money once I earn it?

Entrepreneurship.

There is unlimited possibility and freedom that come from building your own business. When deciding how to plan for your future, start here. Seek God for what business you were created for. Take time to create a mission that explains why you do everything in business. This will help you say no to the wrong opportunities and yes to the right opportunities. Next, start creating your systems and processes, blocking time to work, getting your goods or services out to those who need them, getting paid, and keeping track of your income. Ask God to show you who you should work alongside in business and in what capacity you should work with them. You will need others. Pray for your business daily and learn all you can about the industry you are serving.

Work.

If you choose to work for someone else, treat their dream the way you want others to treat your dream. Work like God is watching you. Your job can fund your dream or business you want to create on your own. Follow the rhythms of God's grace to know when and how to make moves from one job to the next. Being chronically late is a matter of dishonor, so work to show up on time. Have integrity and be kind to those you work with. Work a little more than expected, but not too much more so that you won't burn out. Give 100% effort when you are at your job and take time off to recharge.

Money.

Begin with knowing and deciding that all your money belongs to God; He allows you to manage it. Find an upright church to pay tithes to and ask God to show you how to save, invest, and spend the rest. Learn about finances and how to be wise about this area of life. Work to not allow money to be an idol or a master. Money is to be managed and used to bless. Avoid debt and finance only what can be paid off quickly. Patience will serve you well in your financial life.

Be strategic with how you use credit. Take good care of what you are blessed to buy with the money you earn.

Self.

Managing the business of yourself is essential to being successful in the business of work. Keep up with doctor and dental appointments, medications, exercise, supplements, bills, tax documents, car & home maintenance, insurance policies, paperwork, wardrobe, hygiene, photos, files, hard drives, clouds, wills & POAs, music, shows, movies, credit score, passwords, travel, subscriptions, bank account balances, relationships, and celebrations are just as important as the work you do that makes money. Don't neglect any of these things. Make or take time to see that it all gets done. Poor self-management can lead to losing relationships, reputation and money.

What do you want the next generation to know about the world of work, business, and money?

To the one whom this is passed on to, what do you want the next generation to know about the world of work, business, and money?

To the next one whom this is passed on to, what do you want the next generation to know about work and business?

Section 5:
Being Married

Whom will I marry? How will I find them? How will they find me? How will I know (s)he is the right one?

The Choice.

Choosing to love someone for a lifetime is a special decision that should be made very carefully. The one you choose to marry should be a person you can be your true self around. A person you'd consider marrying should be one you can share your dreams with, and they wholeheartedly support those dreams. You should love them inside and out. Praying for them before you meet them is key, and you must continue to pray for them daily once you meet them. Call on God for them and their needs. Ask Him to show you how to love them best. Take the time to know their love language so you will love them the way they understand and receive love.

By the time you're ready to marry, many of the potential choices that may cross your path will have experienced hardships and trauma that may be keeping them from being who they truly are. You must communicate openly and honestly with them and inquire about their past so that you know who you are really dealing with. Ask God to reveal everything you need to see about a potential spouse. Marry someone because of who they really are and not for who they could become. Choose to marry someone who you enjoy being with more than anyone else and who you can laugh with often. Most importantly, they must believe in Jesus.

The Marriage.

Set a goal to make your spouse's life better and be an example to others for how to be an excellent spouse. You'll need patience, understanding, and a good sense of humor. Plan to have fun together away from work, home, and family. Communicate clearly, often, honestly, and in love as much as possible. Laugh often. Be wise and transparent about finances. Have friends who support your marriage.

Love extended family together but keep them outside of your relationship. Keep God at the center by praying together and knowing what the Bible says about you. Use the words in the Bible to form prayers for your spouse and pray with and over them daily. Invest in your marriage by being intentional to be healthy spiritually, mentally, emotionally, physically, financially, domestically, socially, as a parent, and in appearance. Build something together that will last beyond your marriage. Finally, love and raise your children well, but prioritize a healthy marriage first.

Your Part.

Endeavor to walk a path of lifelong learning, growing, inner healing, and deliverance so that you can show up in your marriage as a healed and whole person. Spend short times alone to rest and be refreshed by God so you can show up at home better. Spoil your spouse and be helpful. Explore and discover new things and places with them. Remember that your happiness is up to you and your joy comes from God, so don't put that responsibility on your spouse. Be intentional about having and being fun.

Do the work to be comfortable in your own skin. Be authentic and confident. Listen to your spouse carefully and remember what they tell you. Be thoughtful, unselfish, and considerate while also clearly communicating your own needs and desires. Find out what they need to thrive and offer that to them. Check in with them often to see what's troubling their heart and mind. Express thankfulness for what they do. Love your spouse well. You are a gift, they are a gift, and a good marriage is a gift. It is worth protecting fiercely.

What do you want the next generation to know about marriage?

To the one whom this is passed on to, what do you want the next generation to know about marriage?

To the next one whom this is passed on to, what do you want the next generation to know about marriage?

Section 6:
Being a Parent

What do I need to know about becoming a parent? What do children need? How can a be a good parent?

Gifts From God.

Children are gifts of life from Heaven, whether you plan for them or not. How you speak about your children is a crucial part of their development, so make certain to only speak words of life about and over them. Teach them about God, His word, how to pray, hear and obey His voice for themselves. Seek God and encourage your children to know their strengths and weaknesses. Give careful thought to what you name your children.

What Children Need.

Children need to be taught and be given the opportunity to practice what they've been taught. They need help, even when they don't think they do. Help them understand how to be resilient and overcome hard times. Nurture their strengths and supply help where they are weak. Have fun: sing, laugh, dance, and play often. Teach them about forgiveness, healthy boundaries, family unity, and having faith. Encourage your children to be who they were created to be and to be that boldly. Listen to them carefully, and discipline from a place of love. Teach them to be wise with money and other people's hearts. Let them see you learning and solving problems and apologizing when you're wrong.

Explain all of life happening around them so that they learn to be aware of their surroundings and have well-rounded social skills. Be honest with them about what they need to know about conditions that run in the family and what you've struggled with. Also, make sure they know what obstacles you've overcome and the talents that their ancestors possessed. Show them how to work smarter and not harder and to staff their lives so they can focus on their purpose. Model how to stay healthy and keep up with medical needs.

Nurturing Children.

Challenge your children to do all they are capable of and celebrate each success they have. Emphasize the importance of reading and writing all throughout life, so they never stop learning, growing, and sharing. Teach them the importance of rest and protecting their mental and emotional health. Tell your children what you like about them and name the positive qualities you notice about them. Allow them the space and opportunity to create all that God has placed them on Earth for so that they leave none of their God-given ideas in their head or in their heart. Children continue to need their parent's prayers and support when they become adults. Leave a legacy for them but teach them how to steward the legacy so that it is not lost for the following generations.

What do you want the next generation to know about being a parent?

To the one this is passed on to, what do you want the next generation to know about being a parent?

To the next one whom this is passed on to, what do you want the next generation to know about being a parent?

Section 7:
Finding & Fighting for Your Purpose

How do I know what my purpose is? Who is connected to my purpose? What do I need to know about living out my purpose?

You.

Your biggest resource is you. There is an enemy in this world, and that enemy wants to destroy you. Read the Bible scriptures that tell what God thinks about you and define your identity by His words only. Protect and invest in your spirit, soul, body, family, home, and intellectual property. This will ensure that your identity will never change even when your status in life does.

God, Time & People.

Spending time with God in prayer and reading His word is how you find and fight for your purpose. Schedule time with God for prayer each morning, read and study the Bible daily, listen to songs about Him, learn how to praise and worship Him, and write down what you hear God tell you. Carve out time to be alone, focus on your health and be with those most important to you. Don't hold grudges. Ask for forgiveness and forgive others quickly. This will free you to be all you're purposed to be. People are God's greatest resource. Find out how you're supposed to be serving people, and your purpose will be attached.

Words.

Watch your words. Speak life only, but don't stay silent. If you say nothing, you'll get nothing. Saying nothing is almost as bad as saying the wrong thing. Make sure to speak up for others when they need a voice and not sympathize with injustice silently. If you're not sure what to say: pray for wisdom, go to the word of God and say what He says, and always speak the truth in love.

What do you want the next generation to know about finding and fighting for your purpose?

To the one whom this is passed on to, what do you want the next generation to know about finding and fighting for your purpose?

To the next one whom this is passed on to, what do you want the next generation to know about discovering and fighting for your purpose?

Section 8:
Family Blessings to Believe For

What blessings has my family enjoyed throughout the generations? What talents run in my blood? What gifts should I believe for that my ancestors benefitted from?

Gifts, Talents & Blessings.

Each family has many gifts, talents, and blessings that we should all appreciate and believe for once we apply the work necessary to develop them. Telling the stories of triumph and victory from our past can fuel the current and future generations with the motivation needed to continue the legacy. Far too many families spend time and energy battling life's challenges and rarely enjoy what may come easily for them to enjoy.

In Every Area.

What physical strengths run in your family? Is your family known for mental strength or having a good sense of humor? Do generosity, entrepreneurship, great cooking skills, or prayer warriors line your family tree? Are there musicians, authors, professors, athletes, preachers, military heroes, or world travelers that you're related to? Tell the next generation about the gifts, talents, and achievements of those who came before them so that they can feel the pride of what their ancestors overcame, conquered, and were blessed to accomplish.

What do you want the next generation to know about generational blessings they can believe for?

To the one whom this is passed on to, what do you want the next generation to know about generational blessings they can believe for?

To the next one whom this is passed on to, what do you want the next generation to know about generational blessings they can believe for?

Section 9:
Patterns of Struggle to Overcome

Why do I struggle with certain sins or deficits?
What did my parents battle with?
How do I begin to overcome what I'm challenged by?

Curses and Struggles.

Each family has generational curses and struggles that have been passed down. It is imperative for these challenges to come to light and not be kept secret. Exposing how other family members have struggled with sin, illness, and other battles takes away their power and will empower future generations to be proactive about their healing and prepare them for and win their own battles.

In Every Area.

Does heart disease, allergies, hormone imbalance, headaches, infertility, or an autoimmune disease run in your family? Have family members battled with depression, learning disabilities, anxiety, schizophrenia, double-mindedness, or anger? Are there trends of poverty, gambling addiction, lack of resources, or debt in your family tree? Is there a history of incest, children born out of wedlock, pornography addiction, or divorce in your family? The next generations must know what they could be up against generationally to break the vicious cycles that may already be in motion to keep them trapped in vicious cycles of sin, illness, and struggle.

What do you want the next generation to know about generational patterns of struggle to overcome?

To the one whom this is passed on to, what do you want the next generation to know about generational patterns of struggle to overcome?

To the next one whom this is passed on to, what do you want the next generation to know about generational patterns of struggle to overcome?

Section 10:
Final Words

You and your ancestors have encountered many experiences, struggles, and successes. One of the most important tasks you can accomplish during your lifetime is to record these things for the generations ahead of you so they can leverage that knowledge to their benefit. Your children and grandchildren don't have to suffer or live lives that lose the progress of the generation before them if they are equipped with the knowledge and wisdom they need from the word of God and the pens of their forefathers.

Being equipped with what is penned within this journal can help them make wise decisions about their health, how they earn money, the thoughts they think, who they marry, how they will process their emotions, what words they choose to speak, the career path they will take, how they will raise their children, when they seek help, and how they will develop a relationship with God. The inevitable obstacles that life will bring do not have to be a surprise to our future generations. They can approach life's opportunities with their eyes wide open because they have the intel that they will need to conquer challenges when they come.

What comes from your pen can equip future generations with the information they need to destroy the enemy's plan for their life while also fueling what will nurture God's perfect plan for their lives. Write down what's in your heart and what you know to be true and pass it on. Then charge your children to repeat the process of recording their knowledge and wisdom for their children on the pages within. Instruct your grandchildren to do the same thing for the generation after that. This is how your bloodline can fulfill its God-ordained destiny and make an impact on the world that will bless your family and others forever. What a beautiful way to leave a legacy behind, display your love and equip your family with a tool for breakthrough, victory, and success.

What final words do you want to leave with the next generation?

To the one whom this is passed on to, what final words do you want to leave with the next generation?

To the next one whom this is passed on to, what do you want the next generation to know about generational patterns of struggle to overcome?

Appendix A
Bible Scriptures to Read and Study

What Bible scriptures do you want the next generation to know and remember?

To the one whom this is passed on to, what Bible scriptures do you want the next generation to know and remember?

To the next one whom this is passed on to, what Bible scriptures do you want the next generation to know and remember?

Appendix B

Motivational Speakers & Bible Teachers, Preacher, and Prophets to Follow

Whose voices and teachings do you want the next generation to listen to and learn from?

To the one whom this is passed on to, whose voices and teachings do you want the next generation to listen to and learn from?

To the next one whom this is passed on to, whose voices and teachings do you want the next generation to listen to and learn from?

Appendix C
Music, Movies & Media to Enjoy

What songs, movies, shows, social media influencers, podcasts, and other media do you want the next generation to listen to and learn from?

To the one whom this is passed on to, what songs, movies, shows, social media influencers, podcasts, and other media do you want the next generation to listen to and learn from?

To the next one whom this is passed on to, whose voices and teachings do you want the next generation to listen to and learn from?

Appendix D

Books, Blogs, & Writings to Read

What books, blogs, and writings do you want the next generation to read and learn from?

To the one whom this is passed on to, what books, blogs, and writings do you want the next generation to read and learn from?

To the next one whom this is passed on to, what books, blogs, and writings do you want the next generation to read and learn from?

Appendix E
Advice & Strategy to Remember

What additional advice and strategy do you want the next generation to take heed to and implement?

To the one whom this is passed on to, what additional advice and strategy do you want the next generation to take heed to and implement?

To the next one whom this is passed on to, additional advice and strategy do you want the next generation to take heed to and implement?

Additional Notes

Additional Notes

Made in the USA
Monee, IL
04 November 2026

67384783R00066